ANNA SCARAVELLA

GARDENS AND LANDSCAPES

ANNA SCARAVELLA
GARDENS AND LANDSCAPES

10 Spaces of Beauty

Photographs by Matteo Carassale
Texts by Bartolomeo Sala

New York · Paris · London · Milan

FOREWORD

GARDENS AS SUBSTANCE

Boasting her fourth book dedicated to "creating gardens," Anna Scaravella, a landscape designer with a degree in Forestry, offers a collection of ten garden projects from the north to the south of Italy, which she designed with passion over thirty years of work. For Anna, the garden is a complex subject, both a part of the surrounding landscape and an extension *en plein air* of the house to which it is connected and of which it is a direct complement. Firstly, it should be observed that the idea of the landscape—here considered as the starting point of the complex and imaginative design journey of every garden—is a cultural notion, difficult to define, as it embraces a number of anthropological and cultural factors, the memory and character of the place, stories and traces of the past, physical and volumetric features, preexisting elements, colors, and smells. It's a "synergic and complex vessel of elements" that, in Anna Scaravella's design research, becomes the object of a highly subjective interpretation whose goal is a new definition of the "garden." Committed to the *substance* more than merely the *form* of the garden, Anna reveals a glossary of different design solutions that respond to the challenges of each case: restoration and protection of the old, repurposing and eco-compatibility, ecology and sustainability, a specific approach to contemporary art and the historical landscape, which every time is treated with deep respect and thorough interpretation.

Anna Scaravella, who describes her gardens as "eclectic, sunny, architectural," displays a deep awareness of the uniqueness of each project, stressing how designing a garden is not just a drawing on paper, but must be followed up on-site and throughout the construction phases, when all sorts of botanical additions and amendments, which were sometimes impossible to foresee during the design phase, have to be included and accounted for.

The gardens that form a virtuous dialogue through the pages of this book, therefore, offer various answers to the many problems faced, to the different features of the places and the homes they complement, forming a multilinear, composite botanical poetics, far from clichés or simply "planting plants." Because building a garden is, above all, an intellectual act.

Gilda Bojardi

INTRODUCTION

LANDSCAPING ITALIAN STYLE

ANNA SCARAVELLA & THE CONTEMPORARY NATURALISTIC GARDEN

Since its very inception, the garden (the very etymology suggests the idea of a "guarded, closed space," an "enclosure") has expressed the human need to impose order on nature. The medieval *hortus conclusus* offering calm and shelter from the outside world; the fountains and water games of the Italian Renaissance gardens; the *parterres de broderie* and chambers of topiary of French formal gardens; the crow's foot layout of certain English landscape gardens, which radiate and incorporate the surrounding countryside; and to an extent, even the perfectly mowed lawns of the typical American suburb—despite their different premises and aesthetic outcomes—are all expressions of a similar desire: the wish to subject nature to human control.[1]

[1] For an excellent discussion of the English-style lawn and its meanings, see the chapter "On the Lawn" by Kris Kozlowski Moore in the catalogue of the exhibition *Garden Futures: Designing with Nature,* eds. Mateo Kries and Viviane Stappmans, Vitra Museum, Weil am Rhein, 2023.
[2] Tim Richardson, *Tom Stuart-Smith: Drawn From the Land* (London: Thames & Hudson, 2021).
[3] See *Garden Futures: Designing with Nature.*
[4] Noël Kingsbury and Claire Takacs, *Wild: The Naturalistic Garden* (London: Phaidon, 2022).

And yet, if one looks at contemporary gardens, these seem to be defined precisely by a programmatic rejection of this anxiety and desire for order. Now that our mastery over nature is, if not complete, at least indisputable, and indeed we have to prepare ourselves for the consequences of what climatologists call the Anthropocene, the garden is in the midst of a "naturalistic turn."[2]

This change has deep roots (Gertrude Jekyll, the mother of the cottage garden as we know it, spoke of "wild gardens" as early as the beginning of the twentieth century) and causes that go well beyond climate change. We no longer live in the France of Louis XIV, where "the very formality of the perfectly manicured gardens of the French Baroque reinforced the ideal of the absolutist ruler as the seat of all power"; and today, even the wealthiest among us struggle to justify armies of gardeners to daily dig, prune, weed out, and fertilize in the Sisyphean effort of maintaining tidy hedges and flower beds.[3] Like any such shift in paradigm, its interpretations also vary greatly. Indeed, while there are those who view the contemporary garden as an ecosystem that should be left to its own devices in an attempt to restore and preserve biodiversity, as is the case with Gilles Clément's "garden in motion," the most influential interpreters of the new naturalistic approach—in particular, Piet Oudolf, the designer behind New York's High Line Park—mainly favor a return to nature that is only partial and mostly aesthetic.

Still, no matter the different results, the fact remains that, as Noël Kingsbury writes in his beautiful *Wild: The Naturalistic Garden*, "planting—the way plants are used and arranged—is changing."[4]

Not only do contemporary gardens—and contemporary green spaces in general—now make extensive use of spontaneous prairies, mixed borders of hardy perennials, and ornamental grasses whose purpose is to artificially create a wild, spontaneous microcosm; for aesthetic as well as practical reasons, they also pay special attention to sustainability, planting varieties that require little maintenance, need less water, and whose growth and decay provide a garden that is beautiful and arresting throughout the year, not just at its climax in late spring.

Anna Scaravella's gardens fit perfectly within this evolution of landscape design. Rather than trying to replicate "an ideal of ordered nature," she seeks plants that adapt to existing conditions, resist drought well, and require little maintenance. When appropriate, she also allows the garden to develop spontaneously; however, she does so from a very different starting point and sensibility.[5]

Graduating with a BA in Forestry from the University of Florence before undergoing a long apprenticeship, initially under the Japanese landscape designer Haruki Miyajima and then as a designer and works supervisor for a famous Tuscan nursery, Scaravella's main inspiration was and remains the Italian landscape, conceived not only as the sum of its morphological, botanical, and climatic characteristics, but as the product of a historical process shaped by human activity over the centuries.

The pages that follow collect ten gardens spanning the whole peninsula from North to South, from Brianza to Apulia, passing through Tuscany and Umbria, to best illustrate this approach to landscape design, which is at once eclectic and site-specific.

At first glance, some of the gardens included here may appear rather classical and almost secondary to the architecture they complement, but in reality they feature important landscape interventions (Albera and Biella), or subtly reference the botanical history of the area (Carimate), or, yet still, while remaining landscape gardens through and through, they adapt to the microclimate and the general rises in temperature that have affected the Po Valley over the past thirty years (Bellaria). Others—rejecting the use of the typical English lawn: "a green desert" that is difficult to maintain, as described by the English garden designer James Hitchmough, and instead embracing a style that alternates mixed borders with shrubs and trees typical of the Mediterranean scrub—are recognizably contemporary in their blend of austerity and exuberance (Elba Island, Ostuni).[6] Still others open like windows onto the surrounding landscape (Capalbio, Passignano), or, behind their lush and romantic appearance, gradually reveal their identity as "gardens in motion" in which native species have been allowed to reclaim what was once barren land (Zucca Uomo, Bagno Vignoni).

---

[5] Kingsbury and Takacs, *Wild*.
[6] See *Garden Futures: Designing with Nature*.

The common feature that brings together these gardens is the sustained dialogue with the surrounding landscape. Over the course of the years, the geometries typical of Italian formal gardens have given way to the aesthetic interplay of native and exotic grasses typical of the naturalistic garden, and mixed borders of hardy perennials and wild prairies that only need to be mowed a couple of times a year have replaced the lawns, the boxwood parterres, and the yew hedges. But this evolution is itself the result of a coherent poetics that always starts with context.

To this end, Scaravella defines as "sustainable" any garden in which plants—be they native or exotic—best adapt to the climate and soil: "Plants that thrive do not need phytosanitary treatments or excessive fertilization, and thus reduce maintenance and impact." Another very important element is resistance to drought and water scarcity, which, as a result of hotter summers and more irregular rainfall, is becoming a constant of the Italian landscape. For this reason—contrary to some landscapes typical of North America and Northern Europe, where the naturalistic garden was born and from which it draws inspiration—prairies and mixed borders are never the dominant element but instead coexist with shrubs and trees, to avoid creating a "wild-looking" garden that is completely disconnected from the surrounding landscape. And this is also why, if there is a true stylistic signature in Anna Scaravella's practice, this is provided by the massive and varied use of her beloved Mediterranean species: the Aleppo pine, cork oak, holm oak, oak, strawberry tree, and tree heather, but also drought-resistant evergreen shrubs such as rosemary and myrtle.

Gardens have always been the expression of ideas and metaphors, an artificial microcosm reflecting power as well as the ideals of a perfect society. The naturalistic garden —even in its most aesthetic and less ecologically oriented expressions—seeks to reverse the relationship of dominion between humans and nature by taking inspiration from the wild prairie and channeling the natural development of the latter. While using plants and embracing influences from all over the world, Anna Scaravella's eclectic garden is by contrast deeply rooted in what always lay beyond the enclosure of the Italian garden: the Italian landscape in all its expressions, from the most agricultural and man-made to the wildest and untamed.

By allowing this landscape to finally break into the garden, at times even conquering it, Anna Scaravella's landscape design shows us a path—the most plausible of many—for Italian gardens of the future.

DESIGNS

TECA HOUSE, BIELLA, PIEDMONT, 2018

A THEATER IN REINFORCED EARTH

Built at the same time as the architecture by Federico Delrosso, the garden of Teca House may at first appear as a minimal intervention accompanying the glass house inspired by Philip Johnson's modernist original. In actual fact, it conceals a sophisticated approach, characterized by the preservation of spontaneously growing plants and earthworks aimed at highlighting the beauty of the house while opening up the view to the surrounding vista dominated by the Ivrea Morainic Amphitheater visible in the distance.

View from above of Teca House with its woodland of Castanea sativa *and* Quercus petraea *to the north and the serpentine that snakes through the prairie, with examples of isolated durmast trees.*

Placed atop the highest hill in the area, and accessible via a serpentine that highlights its scenic location, the house—once the ruin of an old agricultural depot now turned into a fully sustainable and self-sufficient contemporary house thanks to the solar panels installed on the roof—is sheltered to the north by a wood of oak and chestnut trees and to the south by a wild prairie dotted with spontaneous oaks. This southern edge had been infested by bamboo that had colonized it completely. So, instead of devising abstruse geometries and high-maintenance mixed borders, the designer decided with the client to leave everything to the natural wild prairie, making sure the spontaneous oaks grown from seed were also preserved.

The same contemporary logic, which blends good design with sustainability, characterizes the area near the house as well. Since the space was very limited, the decorative and structural elements were thought of as one.

The green barriers, designed to protect from the steep slopes below, are genuine natural parapets made of native shrubs such as dog rose, hawthorn, spindle, and *Hippocrepis emerus*, as well as ornamental berry shrubs. Different types of wild grasses were selected to create a natural prairie landscape at the edges of the wood, while the massive landscaping intervention was concealed and softened by the wild grasses that naturally colonized the reinforced earth walls—in particular, the fern that from the wood slowly infiltrated the gaps between the rocks, the dry-stone walls, and the staircases made from local stones.

Incidentally, most of the garden requires one or two mowings a year, which goes to show how aesthetics and low maintenance are not necessarily mutually exclusive but can go hand in hand.

Northern side of Teca House. The Calamagrostis x acutiflora "Overdam" *and* Trachelospermum asiaticum *insinuate themselves into the rough stone of the staircase. In the background, above the wall, a mixed border of* Berberis thunbergii, Jasminum nudiflorum, *and* Pyracantha "Navaho" *acts as a natural parapet.*

The woodland of durmast and chestnut trees to the north of the garden. The barriers of plants alongside are made up of native species such as Crataegus monogyna, Rosa canina, Euonymus europaeus, Cytisus scoparius, *and decorative shrubs of berries such as* Cotoneaster franchetii, Pyracantha angustifolia, Viburnum tinus.

Opposite
Along the dry-stone staircase grow Pennisetum alopecuroides "Hameln," Calamagrostis x acutiflora "Overdam," Trachelospermum asiaticum, *and the fern* Dryopteris filix-mas, *spontaneous and originating from the adjacent woodland of chestnuts and durmasts.*

Hedera helix *was used as a cascading plant in some sections of the walls. The male fern from the undergrowth is left free to colonize the dry-stone walls.*

The ears of Calamagrostis x acutiflora "Overdam."
At the bottom of Teca House are Gaura lindheimeri *and low-growing grasses,*
Koeleria macrantha, Hakonechloa macra, *and* Carex flacca.

pp. 28–29
The embankment created out of a wall of reinforced earth is bordered to the north by a barrier of plants interrupted by large dry stones, with the grasses Calamagrostis x acutiflora "Overdam" *and* Pennisetum alopecuroides "Hameln."

The spontaneous prairie growing along the avenue that leads up to Teca House. Of very low maintenance (it requires cutting just once or twice a year), it is of great ornamental value, its grasses changing with the seasons.

Opposite
The protective borders of plants on the northern side of the garden. In the background, a magnificent example of Quercus petraea.

TREES
Arbutus unedo
Quercus ilex

SHRUBS, SUBSHRUBS
Berberis thunbergii
Cotinus coggygria
Cotoneaster franchetii
Cotoneaster lacteus
Crataegus monogyna
Cytisus scoparius
Euonymus europaeus
Hippocrepis emerus
Laurus nobilis
Pyracantha angustifolia
Pyracantha "Navaho"
Rosa canina
Viburnum tinus

CLIMBERS
Hedera helix
Jasminum nudiflorum
Trachelospermum asiaticum

GRASSES, PERENNIAL GRASSES
Achillea millefolium
Calamagrostis x acutiflora "Overdam"
Carex flacca
Deschampsia cespitosa
Gaura lindheimeri
Hakonechloa macra
Koeleria macrantha
Pennisetum alopecuroides "Hameln"
Stipa tenuissima

The Teca House woodland at sunset with specimens of Quercus petraea *immediately behind.*

Opposite
Teca House at sunset, with the woods behind. The southern side is supported by a wall in reinforced earth colonized by wild grasses.

CARIMATE [COMO], LOMBARDY, 2013–18

FROM BRIANZA TO THE WORLD

Perhaps the subtlest example of Anna Scaravella's "philological" approach to context, the garden of Carimate dialogues not only with the austere and essential architecture of the house but also with the Brianza landscape—an area historically known for its bold experimentation and botanical curiosity, which climate change and rising temperatures have recently made suitable to Mediterranean and drought-resistant plants that would have been unthinkable a few years ago.

A pruned yew hedge separates the vegetable garden from the lawn. On the opposite side, a sinuous border of evergreen shrubs creates a trompe-l'œil *effect, giving the impression that the garden continues into the coniferous and broad-leaved forest of the Carimate golf course, if not annexing it altogether.*

Upon entering, the visitor is greeted by a vegetable garden bordered by yews and gravel paths, in which the presence of perennial shrubs such as myrtle together with an olive tree prevents the space from appearing barren during the winter months.

This is the only conspicuous "architectural" intervention in a garden that, on the contrary, wants to merge with its surroundings. A low, sinuous border of evergreen shrubs creates a *trompe l'œil* effect, whereby the garden seems to disappear into the wood of coniferous and broadleaved trees of the nearby golf course, previously an eighteenth-century villa. At the same time, the presence of Mediterranean varieties and trees such as strawberry trees and olive trees, or the magnificent cork oak right by the house, a parallelepiped in glass and stone, enriches a garden already made luxuriant by camellias, azaleas, and Japanese cherries, once exotic plants that have since become typical of the large parks of this area.

Brianza is also the place of Anna's first apprenticeship, as she likes to tell. Here she spent her formative years under the guidance of Japanese landscape designer Haruki Miyajima. This early experience introduced her to the rich local nursery tradition, and, in its apparent naturalness and simplicity, the Carimate garden makes full use of this wealth for a result that is beautiful all year round but reaches its peak in autumn, when the colors of the deciduous plants' leaves stand out from the dark green of the conifers and different hues of red, coral, and yellow produce a foliage of rare beauty.

Opposite
Open-air living room furnished with contemporary wooden furniture. In the background, the swimming pool and the northern side of the garden, made up of native and exotic species from all over the world.

pp. 38–39
A single olive tree grows next to the swimming pool. In the background, the shrubby and arboreal scrub of the northwestern side of the garden with laurel, cork tree, beech, Cornus florida "Rubra," Viburnum x bodnantense, *and* Rhododendron "Kure-no-yuki."

The vegetable garden bordered by pruned yew trees and gravel paths. An olive tree and evergreen hedges of Tarentine myrtle border the flower beds. Along the southern and western sides grow white-flowered camellias, Osmanthus fragrans, *and* Hydrangea *with blue and white flowers.*

Opposite
A specimen of Prunus x subhirtella "Autumnalis Rosea." *It is a hybrid of* Prunus incisa x Prunus itosakura, *both of Eastern origin. Tiny bright pink flowers bloom several times from autumn to spring, either before or as the leaves start to grow.*

In sequence, the olive tree, the shrub, and tree scrub of the garden, and the majestic conifers of the golf course, cedars and Pinus sylvestris.

Opposite
The setting of the infinity pool, with stone cladding and wooden slat flooring.

TREES

Acer japonicum
Arbutus unedo
Cupressus sempervirens
Magnolia x loebneri "Leonard Messel"
Olea europaea
Prunus x subhirtella "Autumnalis Rosea"
Quercus suber

SHRUBS, SUBSHRUBS

Abelia x grandiflora
Buxus sempervirens
Camellia japonica "Alba Plena"
Camellia japonica "Alba Simplex"
Camellia japonica "Hagoromo"
Camellia japonica "Nuccio's Gem"
Camellia japonica "Pearl Maxwell"
Camellia sasanqua "Hime Botan"
Camellia sasanqua "Hino de Gumo"
Caryopteris x clandonensis "Heavenly Blue"
Ceratostigma willmottianum
Chimonanthus praecox
Cornus florida "Rubra"
Hydrangea macrophylla "Benelux"
Hydrangea macrophylla "Mariesii Perfecta"
Hydrangea quercifolia "Snow Queen"
Laurus nobilis
Myrtus communis subsp. *tarentina*
Nandina domestica
Osmanthus x burkwoodii
Osmanthus fragrans
Perovskia atriplicifolia "Blue Spire"
Phyllostachys aurea
Phyllostachys bambusoides "Holochrysa"
Phyllostachys bissetii
Phyllostachys nigra f. *punctata*
Pieris japonica
Pittosporum heterophyllum
Rhododendron "Kure-no-yuki"
Rosa "Cornelia"
Rosa "Felicia"
Rosa "Penelope"
Sarcococca ruscifolia
Syringa x laciniata
Taxus x media "Hicksii"
Viburnum x bodnantense
Viburnum carlesii "Compactum"
Viburnum plicatum
f. *tomentosum* "Pink Beauty"

CLIMBERS

Trachelospermum asiaticum

GRASSES, PERENNIAL GRASSES

Convolvulus sabatius
Helleborus atrorubens
Helleborus niger
Helleborus orientalis
Iris japonica
Liriope "Majestic"
Nepeta "Six Hills Giant"

A specimen branching from the base of Quercus suber *has found its ideal environment here, growing with great vigor close to the southern wall of the villa.*

Opposite
The northeastern side of the garden.
The evergreen mixed border with Osmarea x burkwoodii, Pittosporum heterophyllum, Myrtus communis subsp. tarentina, *and* Arbutus unedo. *In the background, the deciduous trees of the golf course.*

pp. 46–49
At sunset, the garden is discreetly illuminated with picket lights placed in the shrubbery and at ground level in the lawn.

VILLA ALBERA, SALVIROLA [CREMONA], LOMBARDY, 1992–94

THE POND & THE POPLAR

Designed in the early 1990s to complement an old Renaissance villa near Crema, the garden of Villa Albera may appear more "traditional" in comparison with other, later gardens. However, with its eclectic use of architectural elements deployed to create a landscape garden, it perfectly embodies Anna Scaravella's idea of landscape design—that is, the idea that a garden must never feel divorced from its context, but rather use the surrounding landscape, seen as the sum of its visual as well as historical characteristics, as its inspiration and point of departure.

The main entrance of Villa Albera on the eastern side. The historical research revealed no records of a previous garden layout. The only preexisting trees, lime and plane trees, are located between the eastern side of the villa and the rural buildings.

The garden is divided into two areas. The first one, in the immediate vicinity of the house, stands out for the learned, almost playful use of both architectural and landscaping elements that together evoke the idea of the garden as a place of wonder and enchantment. “At the time of the project, I had just visited Barcelona, where I was struck by the sculptor Beverly Pepper’s landscape project for the Parc de l’Estació del Nord,” Anna says. And indeed, while the whole garden is characterized by complex patterns of winding topiary hedges and pathways, the western side features a descending terraced roundabout with *Lagerstroemia* at its center. Just beyond, an artificially created hill merges with what is left of the old perimeter wall in an intervention that bridges the gap between romantic ruin and contemporary land art.

However, it is in the area beyond the old garden that the intervention achieves its most refined and fascinating expression. As it stood originally, the property saw a significant imbalance between the house and the garden, which was squeezed between the boundary walls, the old chapel, and agricultural buildings on the eastern side. For this reason, the designer convinced the client to acquire an additional one-and-a-quarter-acre agricultural plot on the northern side and inserted there a long pond, 115 feet long and 10 feet wide, which naturally directs the eye toward a group of six cypress poplars arranged in a funnel shape.

Flanked on both sides by a wood planted with trees typical to this area of the Po Valley—such as English oaks, hornbeams, ash trees, and black alders—this trick of perspective opens the view onto the surrounding countryside. By sampling and re-imagining its “grammar,” this garden is the best homage to the Crema landscape —to the special poetry of its poplar groves (indeed, “Albera” is the word for poplar in the local dialect), and its canals and waterways that, beginning in late autumn, seem to almost fade and disappear into the fog.

An ancient stucco portal opens onto the driveway that leads to the eastern side of the villa.

View from above of the villa and the park. A long pool of water connects the area near the house–where classic elements of the "Italian" garden and the landscape garden are interpreted freely–with the portion of the garden to the north, formerly used for agriculture, which is bordered by a woodland of species typical to the Po Valley, such as Quercus robur, Carpinus betulus, *and* Fraxinus excelsior.

pp. 56 and 57
The eastern side of the building restored by architect Maurizio Camillo Sala. A box hedge defines the square in front of the double entrance staircase. After the renovation of the garden, the preexisting lime and plane trees have been maintained and are no longer cut so drastically as in the past.

The pillars of the portico facing the eastern side of the building are covered in a climbing Rosa "Exploit."

Opposite
The multi-arched porticoes of the buildings on the eastern side offer a splendid view of the villa.

pp. 60 and 61
The square in front of the southern entrance of Villa Albera was created with a brick design combined with Botticino stone and bush-hammered serizzo.

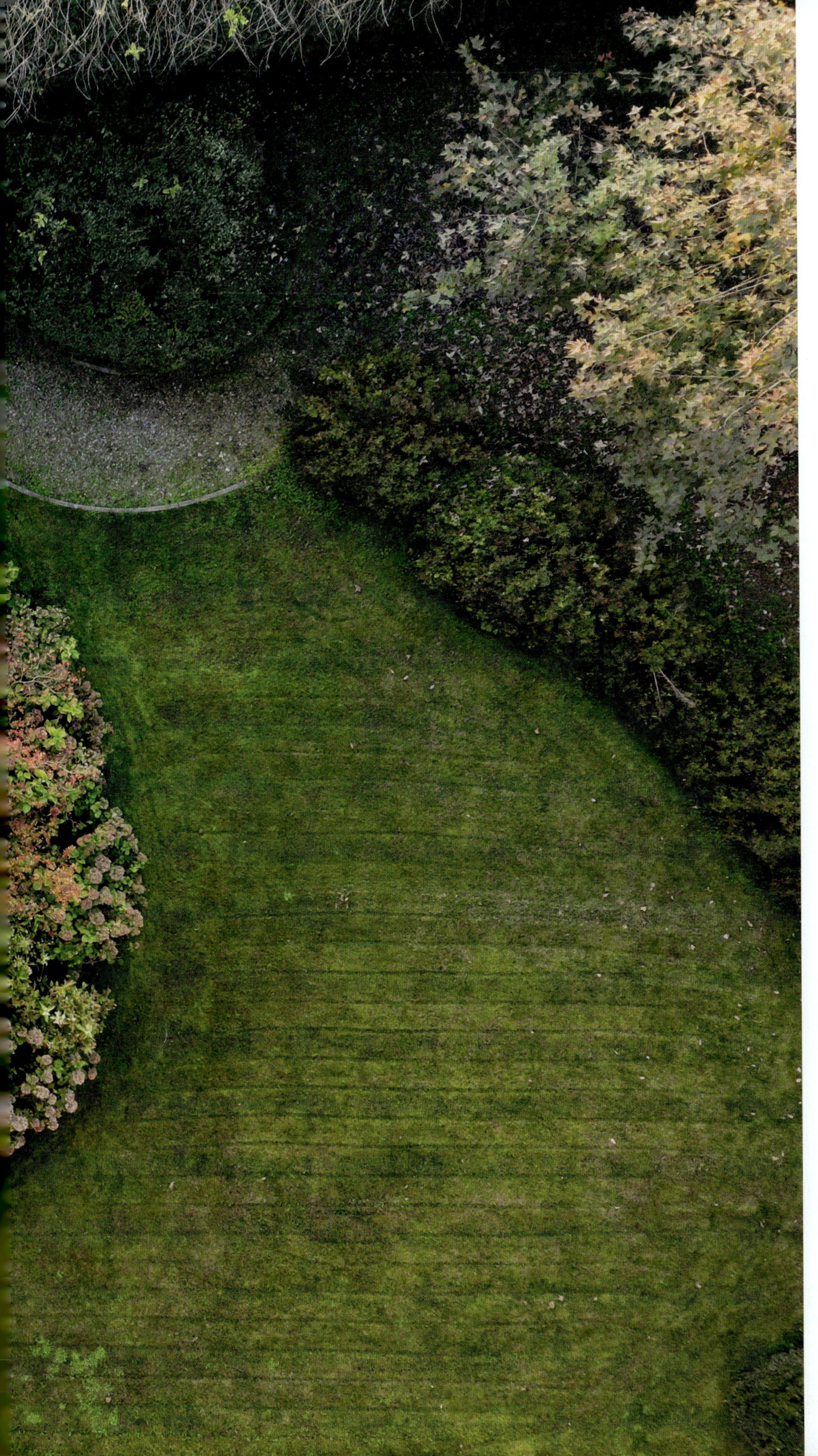

On the western side of the villa, the terraced rotunda was conceived as a play of concentric floors to increase the limited space between the villa and the perimeter border wall. Along the south and west sides, a sinuous gravel driveway is defined by shaped concrete curbs.

The landscaping work undertaken revealed the old terracotta brick icehouse.

Opposite
A Lagerstroemia indica *tree with a very distinctive trunk emerges from the central circle of the lowest terraced rotunda. A border of* Hydrangea macrophylla *now grows on the middle floor.*

pp. 66–67
The pool that runs in line with the northern side of the building.
A specimen of Paulownia tomentosa *marks the eastern limit of the artificial hill.*

Detail of the design where the artificial hill begins. The edge of the villa's pavement marks the center of a circle where slices of concrete radially alternate with slices of lawn, surrounded by a curvilinear box hedge.

Opposite
The artificial hill with Paulownia, *English oak, Po Valley oak, and maple trees, bordered on the northern and western sides by a gravel driveway.*

pp. 70 and 71
The pool, a reinterpretation of the many canals that distinguish the Crema landscape, runs through the garden and directs the gaze toward the horizon at the edge of the fields. The cypress poplars, arranged in a funnel shape, act as a connecting element with the landscape. Terracotta vases with boxwood topiary are placed along the southern side of the pool, which is bordered by slabs of concrete.

TREES
Acer campestre
Acer pseudoplatanus
Alnus glutinosa
Carpinus betulus
Carpinus betulus "Fastigiata"
Crataegus laevigata
Ficus carica
Fraxinus excelsior
Koelreuteria paniculata
Lagerstroemia indica "Rosea"
Paulownia tomentosa
Populus nigra "Italica"
Prunus avium
Punica granatum
Quercus robur
Taxus baccata
Salix babylonica

SHRUBS, SUBSHRUBS
Abelia x grandiflora
Buxus sempervirens
Cornus mas
Corylus avellana
Exochorda racemosa
Hibiscus syriacus
Hydrangea arborescens "Annabelle"
Laurus nobilis
Osmanthus x burkwoodii
Osmanthus heterophyllus
Philadelphus "Belle Etoile"
Photinia serratifolia
Rosa "Cornelia"
Rosa "Felicia"
Rosa "Penelope"
Rosmarinus officinalis
Spiraea "Arguta"
Spiraea x vanhouttei
Syringa vulgaris
Viburnum x burkwoodii
Viburnum opulus
Viburnum tinus
Weigela "Bristol Ruby"

CLIMBERS
Campsis grandiflora
Clematis montana var. *rubens*
Hedera helix
Hydrangea petiolaris
Lonicera periclymenum
Parthenocissus tricuspidata "Veitchii"
Rosa "Albéric Barbier"
Rosa banksiae "Lutea"
Rosa "Clair Matin"
Rosa "Dorothy Perkins"
Rosa "Exploit"
Rosa "New Dawn"
Trachelospermum jasminoides
Wisteria sinensis

GRASSES, PERENNIAL GRASSES
Bergenia cordifolia
Hemerocallis "Flaming Sunset"
Ophiopogon japonicus

A detail of the wonderful, twisted branches of the Lagerstroemia *in the terraced rotunda.*

Opposite
The rural buildings located on the eastern side of the villa are completely covered by the autumn Canadian vine.

VILLA BELLARIA, RIVERGARO [PIACENZA], EMILIA ROMAGNA, 1993–2002

TROPICAL VIBES IN THE PO VALLEY

Designed at the same time as Villa Albera, the garden of Villa Bellaria draws from and foregrounds the romantic spirit of the villa as it was originally conceived. It complements the winding serpentine paths, picturesque nooks, and exotic species of the original garden with the introduction of typically Mediterranean, drought-resistant plants that, although once considered an anomaly in this area, have instead adapted well to the temperate and moderately dry microclimate of Piacenza's hills.

The main driveway with a double row of Pinus pinea.
On the terraced level, the crescent-shaped vegetable garden is defined by boxwood hedges demarcating the flower beds. In the background, centennial cypresses and Lebanon cedars with their characteristic crowns and inclined, tabular tops.

The layout of the garden, which has been largely preserved, dates back to the early twentieth century, when the original owner—formerly an Italian consul in Africa and a keen collector of tropical plants—decided to create in this place, where the Po Valley meets the first hills, his own little oasis in which to experiment with Mediterranean as well as exotic varieties. The Lebanon cedars, stone pines, olive trees, strawberry trees, cypresses, laurels, and palms were planted at that time. However, years of neglect reduced the garden to a jungle. "When we started to work on the project," Anna remembers, "the villa had been abandoned for more than fifteen years and black locust trees, palms, and laurel trees grown spontaneously from seed had taken over and erased the flower beds and pathways."

Much of the work then consisted in revealing the design of the old paths, as well as complementing the already existing trees and shrubs with a rich collection of perennial grasses and drought-resistant Mediterranean species that would suit the context; over the following years, they have adapted well to the changing climate. Romantic and slightly extravagant touches like the amoeba-shaped pond were balanced by the introduction of classical elements typical of Italian formal gardens, such as hedges of boxwood and spontaneous laurels, which, when trimmed and shaped according to various topiary forms, replicated instead the sinuous serpentines of English landscape gardens.

Arranged around three areas—two of which were preexisting, the third the result of substantial earthworks—the garden stands out for its variety of plants and botanical richness. In its more sun-exposed south side, the garden features mixed borders alternating Mediterranean aromatics such as rosemary with roses, irises, peonies, and exotic species. To its north, shaded by cedars and other centennial trees, it hosts ferns, acanthus, lily turfs, and a collection of other shade-loving plants. Finally, two pergolas, both covered by preexisting grapevines, lead to the newly built swimming pool bordered by a mixed hedge of native shrubs and trees such as oak and field maple; the resulting effect is the garden appearing to fade away into the surrounding landscape.

Opposite
Two specimens of Trachycarpus fortunei *palms.* Solanum jasminoides "Album" *climb the metal-framed Tuscan terracotta vases. In the background, the northern side of Villa Bellaria covered in Canadian vine.*

pp. 78–79
The ancient, amoeba-shaped pool with fish and water lilies. In the background, Trachelospermum jasminoides *and* Parthenocissus tricuspidata "Veitchii" *envelop the annex.*

At the bottom of the polycormic specimen of Eriobotrya japonica *is a parterre of boxwood pruned into spheres.*

Opposite
Acanthus mollis *in bloom. Mixed borders of shade-loving plants such as* Helleborus, Geranium, Hosta, Liriope, *and ferns have found the perfect conditions below the majestic Lebanon cedars and along the winding paths.*

Boxwood topiary against a backdrop of succulents grown in pots, which are moved to the greenhouse during the winter months.

Opposite
The gate on the western border of the garden opens onto a vineyard of Merlot grapes. In the background, the Trebbia River and the gentle hilly landscape overlooking the Po Valley.

Mixed border of Tulbaghia violacea, Gaura lindheimeri, Lychnis coronaria, Perovskia atriplicifolia "Blue Spire," *and* Artemisia arborescens "Porquerolles." *The two terraced levels built to host the swimming pool area to the north are home to a collection of Mediterranean and drought-resistant plants.*

Opposite
One of the two pergolas that lead from the north side of the garden to the newly built swimming pool. The four rows of vines from the old orchard have been maintained and are supported by simple iron arches.

pp. 86–87
The setting of the swimming pool: the old orchard was transformed into two terraced levels by a significant reinforced concrete retaining wall, covered with ancient local stones. The old orchard in the upper terrace was maintained and improved, while below, the classically shaped swimming pool is framed by a large lawn and mixed Mediterranean borders.

The entrance to the old greenhouse, where citrus trees and succulent plants are sheltered in winter. In the foreground, Hemerocallis *with a carpet of verbena.*

Opposite
View from above of the garden of Villa Bellaria. The hedges bordering the pool area are made up of native species such as Crataegus monogyna, Cornus sanguinea, Prunus spinosa, *and spontaneous seed-born* Laurus nobilis *that has found its ideal environment here. The oaks and field maples grown from seed in the hedge have been maintained, creating a visual continuity with the woods beyond the swimming pool.*

The crescent-shaped vegetable garden is bordered by hedges and spheres of boxwood. A majestic Cupressus sempervirens *and a centenarian specimen of* Arbutus unedo *stand in the background.*

Opposite
Detail of the vegetable garden, looked after by the landlady. Vegetables are planted both in autumn and spring.

p. 92
The main access to Villa Bellaria with a double row of Pinus pinea*. To each side of the avenue lie a border of* Iris *and the hedge of laurel and native shrubs that runs around the entire park.*

p. 93
Geometric flower beds with a collection of Hemerocallis *and* Iris *in the prairie on the southeastern side of the garden.*

pp. 94–95
The exedra in front of the house offers an enchanting view of the southern side of the garden, which is the area with the most favorable microclimate. The gravel paths are lined by mixed borders rich in Mediterranean and exotic drought-resistant species such as Cistus, Phlomis, Santolina chamaecyparissus, Salvia farinacea, *and* Stachys bizantina "Silver Carpet" *alongside roses,* Iris, *and peonies.*

In the foreground, Centranthus ruber *and* Danae racemosa. *In the background, topiary with spheres of boxwood and naturally seeded laurel spheres act as a counterpoint to the mixed borders.*

Opposite
A mixed border of aromatic herbs, Artemisia, Iris, *and* Ceratostigma willmottianum; *in the background, the south side wall of the villa entirely covered with* Trachelospermum jasminoides *and pomegranate tree.*

The western border featuring a laurel topiary pruned into spheres, alongside an undulating laurel hedge.

Opposite

In the garden, fluted terracotta columns that used to adorn the walkways have been maintained and restored. In the background, the avenue of pines with the prairie and geometric flower beds of Iris *and* Hemerocallis*.*

pp. 100–101

The sculptural trunks of the stone pines and a hedge of native shrubs. A laurel exedra marks the southern border of the garden, beyond which lies a deciduous oak forest.

Spheres of boxwood and laurel line the straight path leading to the laurel exedra.

Opposite
A straight driveway in axis with the villa leads to the exedra of pruned laurel on the southern side of the garden. There, a sinuous topiary of laurel and boxwood spheres envelops the iron benches of the belvedere.

TREES

Acer campestre
Aesculus hippocastanum
Arbutus unedo
Catalpa bignonioides
Clerodendrum trichotomum
Cupressus sempervirens
Eriobotrya japonica
Ficus carica
Juglans regia
Lagerstroemia indica
Magnolia grandiflora
Morus alba
Morus nigra
Morus platanifolia
Olea europaea
Paulownia tomentosa
Punica granatum
Quercus pubescens
Taxus baccata

SHRUBS, SUBSHRUBS

Buxus sempervirens
Buxus sempervirens "Rotundifolia"
Caryopteris x clandonensis
Caryopteris x clandonensis "Heavenly Blue"
Caryopteris x clandonensis "Kew Blue"
Ceanothus "Italian Skies"
Ceanothus "Skylark"
Ceanothus thyrsiflorus var. *repens*
Ceratostigma griffithii
Ceratostigma willmottianum
Chimonanthus praecox
Choisya ternata
Cistus albidus
Cistus x purpureus
Cistus x skanbergii
Citrus limon
Citrus trifoliata
Cornus sanguinea
Corylus avellana
Crataegus monogyna
Danae racemosa
Deutzia x magnifica "Staphyleoides"
Exochorda racemosa
Genista lydia
Helichrysum italicum subsp. *serotinum*
Hibiscus moscheutos "Southern Belle"
Hibiscus syriacus
Hydrangea arborescens "Annabelle"
Hydrangea macrophylla "Ayesha"
Hydrangea macrophylla "Mariesii"
Hydrangea macrophylla "M.me E. Mouillère"
Hydrangea macrophylla "Soeur Thérèse"
Hydrangea macrophylla "Tovelit"
Hydrangea paniculata "Grandiflora"
Hydrangea paniculata "Kyushu"
Hydrangea paniculata "Unique"
Hydrangea quercifolia
Laurus nobilis
Lavandula angustifolia
Lavandula angustifolia "Munstead"
Ligustrum japonicum
Nerium oleander
Origanum majorana
Osmanthus heterophyllus
Paeonia x suffruticosa "Yachiyo-tsubaki"
Paeonia x suffruticosa "Yae-zakura"
Paeonia ludlowii
Perovskia atriplicifolia "Blue Spire"
Philadelphus coronarius
Phlomis italica
Phlomis purpurea
Phyllostachys aurea
Prunus spinosa
Rhaphiolepis indica "Springtime"
Rosa "Abraham Derby"
Rosa "Berenice"
Rosa "Brother Cadfael"
Rosa "Buff Beauty"
Rosa "Cardinal de Richelieu"
Rosa "Constance Spry"
Rosa "Cornelia"
Rosa "Eglantyne"
Rosa "Felicia"
Rosa "Glamis Castle"
Rosa "Gertrude Jekyll"
Rosa "Marguerite Hilling"
Rosa "Nevada"
Rosa x odorata "Pallida"
Rosa x odorata "Sanguinea"
Rosa "Othello"
Rosa "Sally Holmes"
Rosa "Tuscany"
Rosa "White Meidiland"
Rosmarinus officinalis
Rosmarinus officinalis "Jackman's Prostratus"
Rosmarinus officinalis "Majorca Pink"
Ruta graveolens
Salvia officinalis
Santolina chamaecyparissus
Sarcococca ruscifolia
Sasa veitchii
Spiraea "Arguta"
Syringa x laciniata
Syringa vulgaris
Teucrium fruticans
Teucrium fruticans "Azureum"
Thymus "Porlock"
Thymus pulegioides
Thymus serpyllum
Thymus serpyllum var. *albus*
Viburnum x bodnantense
Viburnum x burkwoodii
Viburnum opulus
Viburnum plicatum f. *plicatum* "Grandiflorum"
Viburnum plicatum f. *tomentosum* "Lanarth"
Viburnum plicatum f. *tomentosum* "Mariesii"
Viburnum tinus
Vitex agnus-castus

CLIMBERS
Parthenocissus tricuspidata "Veitchii"
Passiflora edulis
Rosa "Albéric Barbier"
Rosa banksiae "Lutea"
Rosa "Climbing Pompon de Paris"
Rosa "Dorothy Perkins"
Rosa "Mermaid"
Rosa "New Dawn"
Rosa "Pierre de Ronsard"
Rosa "Zéphirine Drouhin"
Solanum jasminoides "Album"
Trachelospermum jasminoides
Wisteria sinensis

GRASSES, PERENNIAL GRASSES
Agapanthus campanulatus
Alchemilla mollis
Anemone x hybrida "Honorine Jobert"
Anemone x hybrida "September Charm"
Anemone x hybrida "Whirlwind"
Anemone pulsatilla "Rubra"
Anemone sylvestris
Anemone vitifolia
Aquilegia coerulea
Artemisia arborescens "Porquerolles"
Artemisia dracunculus
Artemisia "Powis Castle"
Athyrium filix-femina
Begonia discolor
Bergenia cordifolia "Purpurea"
Campanula lactiflora "Loddon Anna"
Campanula persicifolia
Campanula persicifolia var. *alba*
Campanula persicifolia "Telham Beauty"
Campanula portenschlagiana
Centranthus ruber
Centranthus ruber var. *coccineus*
Convallaria majalis
Cyclamen hederifolium
Cyclamen purpurascens
Dicentra spectabilis
Dicentra spectabilis "Alba"
Dryopteris filix-mas
Galanthus nivalis
Geranium "Johnson's Blue"
Geranium nodosum
Geranium platypetalum
Helleborus argutifolius
Helleborus niger
Helleborus orientalis
Hemerocallis "Batuffolo"
Hemerocallis "Carved Ivory"
Hemerocallis "Corky"
Hemerocallis "Fiocco Rosa"
Hemerocallis "Fond Caress"
Hemerocallis lilioasphodelus
Hemerocallis "Luxury Lace"
Hemerocallis "May Hall"
Hemerocallis "Pink Charm"
Hemerocallis "Primo Amore"
Hemerocallis "Solleone"
Hesperis matronalis
Heuchera sanguinea
Heuchera villosa "Palace Purple"
Hosta fortunei var. *albopicta*
Hosta fortunei var. *aureomarginata*
Hosta plantaginea
Hosta sieboldiana
Hosta sieboldiana var. *elegans*
Iberis sempervirens
Iris foetidissima
Iris germanica
Kniphofia uvaria
Liriope muscari
Lychnis coronaria
Lychnis coronaria "Alba"
Malva sylvestris "Brave Heart"
Mentha requienii
Nepeta x faassenii
Nepeta racemosa "Superba"
Nepeta "Six Hills Giant"
Ophiopogon japonicus
Paeonia lactiflora
Paeonia lactiflora "Duchesse de Nemours"
Paeonia lactiflora "Sarah Bernhardt"
Platycodon grandiflorus "Albus"
Polygonatum multiflorum
Polystichum aculeatum
Salvia farinacea
Scilla siberica
Sedum spectabile
Stachys byzantina "Silver Carpet"
Tradescantia andersoniana "Osprey"
Verbena bonariensis
Veronica spicata
Vinca major
Vinca minor
Vinca minor f. *alba*
Zantedeschia aethiopica

ZUCCA UOMO, TRAVO [PIACENZA], EMILIA ROMAGNA, 2007–09

THE ESCARPMENT & THE BROOM

The result of a landscaping intervention extending over five acres which from the house came to include the surrounding slopes and hillside, the garden of Zucca Uomo, in the high hills of Piacenza, is a testament to the regenerative power inherent in Anna Scaravella's approach to landscape design, as well as her profound agronomic knowledge of plants, microclimates, and soils which allows her to get the best out of the most difficult and rugged contexts.

Aerial view of Zucca Uomo. The immediate surroundings of the estate buildings consist of a terraced level with large gravel areas and a small, irrigated lawn flanked by a mixed border of roses "Felicia," "Buff Beauty," "Marguerite Hilling," and "Sally Holmes" *and drought-resistant plants.*

This book features some previously neglected gardens and barren and suffering landscapes, but none of these come close to the state of Zucca Uomo in 2007: a "lunar" landscape made of ill-advised earthworks, PVC sheets, and white boulders. Following the client's wishes, near the house the garden has today a small lawn and an especially complex and refined mixed border in which different rose varieties alternate with patches of irises and drought-resistant shrubs such as cotton lavender, Pseudodictamnus, *Salvia*, and sagebrush.

However, it is moving away from the house and venturing along the winding paths that extend all around that visitors can start to appreciate the sensitivity of the intervention, which, in addition to "restoring" the garden to its surrounding landscape, had to take into account the lack of water and the significant jumps in temperature across the different seasons. What was once bare earth and stone is now a mixture of native trees such as oaks, field maples, and flowering ash trees; native shrubs, broom in particular, which has colonized the slopes; and the wild prairie, in part preserved and in part grown from seed.

The latter required a great deal of "philological" research, as no "rustic blend" of this kind was commercially available. For this reason, the designer enlisted the help of a local botanist who, with meticulous care, continues to collect and catalog the species from this area of the Apennines. Balancing out these rougher, wilder elements are a few perks that make a retreat to the countryside "a pleasant escape": the vegetable garden fenced by a hedge of rosemary, the olive grove, the fruit orchard, the chestnut-wood pergolas, and, last but not least, the iron pergola that the owner playfully renamed "the Parthenon," which offers a beautiful view of the surrounding oak woods, meadows, and fields.

Opposite
The driveway to the estate. The main house is surrounded to the north by a border of drought-resistant plants, Laurus nobilis, Arbutus unedo, Viburnum tinus, *and* Pittosporum heterophyllum, *with roses,* Iris, *and* Salvia microphylla *below.*

pp. 110–111
The Zucca Uomo estate with its forest, farmed fields, and prairies. The landscape intervention encompassed an area of five acres that was previously devoid of all vegetation due to prior earthmoving works.

The large chestnut wood pergola on the east side of the house shaded by Wisteria sinesis; *to the sides,* Hydrangea arborescens "Annabelle." *The wall of the house is covered by* "Parkdirektor Riggers" *rose.*

Opposite
The west side of the manor house covered in climbing roses, "New Dawn," "Nahema," *and* Trachelospermum jasminoides.

pp. 114–115
The terrace floor on the same level as the house is marked by a mixed border of roses, Iris, Nepeta, Salvia microphylla, Pseudodictamnus mediterraneus, Cerastium tomentosum, *buddleia, and broom which continues down the slope.*

The large iron pergola, which the owner refers to as "The Parthenon," is a restored antique artifact embellished by rambling roses such as filipes "Kiftsgate," "Paul's Himalayan Musk," *and* "Rambling Rector."

"The Parthenon," which is set as a lookout at the highest point of the estate, offers a magnificent view of the surrounding landscape. Next to it, an isolated specimen of Quercus pubescens, *a species typical of the oak coppiced woods of the area.*

Detail of Spartium junceum, *which was widely used to colonize the steepest and most barren slopes of the estate.*

Opposite
The barren slopes below "The Parthenon" were replanted with Spartium junceum, Cistus, Teucrium fruticans, Helichrysum italicum subsp. serotinum, Artemisia absinthium, and Lavandula angustifolia.

Detail of Artemisia absinthium, *a native species whose natural renewal helps thicken mixed drought-resistant edges.*

pp. 120–121
The garden merges with the woods and prairies. Renaturalization of the area included downy oak, field maple, manna ash, peraster; as for the shrubs, Spartium junceum, Cornus sanguinea, Euonymus europaeus, Prunus spinosa, *and* Rosa canina.

TREES
Acer campestre
Arbutus unedo
Cercis siliquastrum f. *albida*
Crataegus laevigata
Crataegus x media "Paul's Scarlet"
Diospyros kaki
Ficus carica
Fraxinus ornus
Juglans regia
Koelreuteria paniculata
Mespilus germanica
Morus alba
Morus alba "Fruitless"
Olea europaea
Paulownia tomentosa
Punica granatum
Pyrus communis
Pyrus communis "Beech Hill"
Quercus pubescens
Sorbus domestica
Sorbus torminalis
Tilia cordata
Ziziphus jujuba

SHRUBS, SUBSHRUBS
Arbutus unedo "Compacta"
Buddleja alternifolia
Buddleja davidii "Black Knight"
Buddleja davidii "Nanho Blue"
Caryopteris x clandonensis "Heavenly Blue"
Caryopteris x clandonensis "Kew Bleu"
Ceanothus x burkwoodii
Ceanothus "Concha"
Ceanothus x delileanus "Gloire de Versailles"
Ceanothus griseus var. *horizontalis* "Yankee Point"
Ceanothus "Italian Skies"
Ceanothus prostratus
Ceanothus thyrsiflorus var. *repens*
Ceratostigma griffithii
Choisya ternata
Cistus x purpureus
Cistus x skanbergii
Citrus trifoliata
Cornus sanguinea
Cotinus coggygria
Crataegus monogyna
Euonymus europaeus
Genista lydia
Genista "Porlock"
Helichrysum italicum subsp. *serotinum*
Hippocrepis emerus
Hydrangea arborescens "Annabelle"
Hydrangea paniculata "Unique"
Laurus nobilis
Lavandula angustifolia
Malva x clementii "Rosea"
Medicago arborea
Myrtus communis
Osmanthus x burkwoodii
Perovskia atriplicifolia "Blue Spire"
Philadelphus "Belle Etoile"
Pistacia lentiscus
Pittosporum heterophyllum
Prunus spinosa
Pseudodictamnus mediterraneus
Rhaphiolepis indica "Springtime"
Rosa "Ametista"
Rosa "Ardoisée de Lyon"
Rosa "A Shropshire Lad"
Rosa "Ballerina"
Rosa "Baronne Prévost""
Rosa "Belinda"
Rosa "Berenice"
Rosa "Blanc Double de Coubert"
Rosa "Buff Beauty"
Rosa canina
Rosa "Cardinal Hume"
Rosa "Carolina Linnaeus"
Rosa "Charles de Mills"
Rosa "Complicata"
Rosa "Comtesse Cécile de Chabrillant"
Rosa "Cornelia"
Rosa "Eglantyne"
Rosa "Enfant de France"
Rosa "Felicia"
Rosa foetida "Bicolor"
Rosa "Gertrude Jekyll"
Rosa "Hansa"
Rosa "Heritage"
Rosa "Hermosa"
Rosa "Hot Cocoa"
Rosa "Iceberg"
Rosa "Ice Meidiland"
Rosa "James Galway"
Rosa "Marguerite Hilling"
Rosa "Mme Ernest Calvat"
Rosa "Mozart"
Rosa "Neige d'Été"
Rosa "Nevada"
Rosa "Old Blush"
Rosa "Papa Meilland"
Rosa "Penelope"
Rosa "Redouté"
Rosa "Reine des Violettes"
Rosa "Sally Holmes"
Rosa "Sarah van Fleet"
Rosa "Tapis Volant"
Rosa "The Alnwick Rose"
Rosa "The Prince"
Rosa "William Shakespeare"
Rosa "Winchester Cathedral"
Rosa "Yolande d'Aragon"
Rosa "Yves Piaget"
Rosmarinus officinalis
Rosmarinus officinalis "Rampant Boule"
Salix caprea
Salvia microphylla
Santolina chamaecyparissus
Satureja montana
Spartium junceum
Syringa x laciniata
Syringa pubescens subsp. *microphylla* "Superba"
Syringa vulgaris
Teucrium fruticans
Thymus "Porlock"
Thymus serpyllum
Viburnum tinus
Vitex agnus-castus

CLIMBERS
Clematis armandii
Hedera helix
Jasminum nudiflorum
Jasminum officinale
Rosa banksiae "Lutea"
Rosa "Clair Matin"
Rosa "Coral Dawn"
Rosa "Crimson Glory"
Rosa "Crown Princess Margareta"
Rosa "Iceberg Climbing"
Rosa filipes "Kiftsgate"
Rosa laevigata
Rosa "Madame Isaac Péreire"
Rosa "Mermaid"
Rosa "Nahema"
Rosa "Noella Nabonnand"
Rosa "Parkdirektor Riggers"
Rosa "Paul's Himalayan Musk"
Rosa "Pierre de Ronsard"
Rosa "Rambling Rector"
Rosa sempervirens
Rosa "Senateur La Follette"
Rosa "Souvenir d'Alphonse Lavallée"
Rosa "Souvenir de Claudius Denoyel"
Rosa "Souvenir du Docteur Jamain"
Rosa "Teasing Georgia"
Trachelospermum asiaticum
Trachelospermum jasminoides
Vitis vinifera "Almeria"
Vitis vinifera "Dorbli di Darkaia"
Vitis vinifera "Lattuario"
Vitis vinifera "Moscato d'Amburgo"
Vitis vinifera '"Moscato Fior d'Arancio"
Vitis vinifera "Regina di Firenze"
Vitis vinifera "S. Anna di Lipsia"
Vitis vinifera "Sultanina Bianca"
Vitis vinifera "Zibibbo"
Wisteria sinensis

GRASSES, PERENNIAL GRASSES
Artemisia absinthium
Artemisia arborescens "Porquerolles"
Artemisia "Powis Castle"
Aster cordifolius "Little Carlow"
Centranthus ruber
Cerastium tomentosum
Erigeron karvinskianus
Gaura lindheimeri
Geranium "Johnson's Blue"
Iris germanica
Iris "Grand Waltz"
Iris "Laced Cotton"
Iris "Last Call"
Iris "Purple Pepper"
Iris "Salomon Dream"
Iris "Somptuosus"
Iris "Song of Spring"
Iris "Story Book"
Nepeta racemosa "Superba"
Nepeta racemosa "Walker's Low"
Tulbaghia violacea

Lavender envelops an iron bird cage.

pp. 124–125
The pergola of the vegetable garden is interwoven with different varieties of table grapes: "Almeria," "Fior d'Arancio," "Regina di Firenze," *and* "Sultanina Bianca." *At the base there is a border of* Iris; *the vegetable beds alternate with cut roses. The rectangular garden is bordered by a hedge of rosemary.*

BAGNO VIGNONI [SIENA], TUSCANY, 1989-90

THE WOOD BEYOND THE HEDGE

Directly overlooking the famous Etrusco-Roman thermal baths, whose rarefied and almost immobile atmosphere has fascinated poets and artists from Ovid and Montaigne all the way to Tarkovsky, the garden of Bagno Vignoni pays tribute to the landscape of the Val d'Orcia, with its olive groves and wild woods. It is also a fine example of a "garden in motion" that mimics nature by imagining how it would have behaved if left to its own devices in a context characterized by anthropization, in which the landscape itself is the product of centuries of human activity.

The Etrusco-Roman thermal bath overlooked by the house and garden of Bagno Vignoni.
In the background, the typical Val d'Orcia landscape with olive groves, woods, and prairies.

In the early 1990s, the garden was desolate and barren, the result of a previous intervention that failed to take into account the specificities of the place, such as the presence of Sienese clay (a difficult soil to which few plants can adapt) and the lack of water due to low rainfall. There were two possible paths ahead: go for the obvious choice and opt for a classic Tuscan formal garden with cypresses and boxwood topiaries, or instead venture down the more daring path and create an evocative landscape garden inspired by the Mediterranean species native to the area, which would merge with the surroundings.

A low hedge of laurustinus demarcates the old stone house, which dates back to the fourteenth century, and allows the visitor to take in the view of the thermal pool. From there, the garden starts to ascend in a rather limited space. The lawn and pathways, made of stones reclaimed from old village pavings, snake through mixed borders of lavender, rosemary, and tree germander. The olive trees soon give way to a slope covered in drought-resistant low shrubs and trees typical of Val d'Orcia, such as holm oaks, field maples, strawberry trees, and, in particular, the downy oak, which farmers in the area would use both for its acorns to feed their pigs and for firewood to heat their homes during the winter. Beyond this artificial "microwood" is an orchard, where various fruit trees and berry bushes grow in a bedding of wild grasses that, once mowed, serve as natural mulch.

"The idea was Alighiero's" (the gardener who succeeded his father in the management of the garden and now tends to it with loving care). "Maintenance is much lower compared to a conventional garden," Anna explains. "So much so that there is no need for an automatic irrigation system." The impression is not one of studied and exhibited austerity, however. On the contrary, the visual impact—especially at dawn, when the garden is shrouded in mist—reveals a romantic, almost luxuriant soul, highlighted by the many resting areas with cast-iron benches and amenities such as a boules court of the utmost simplicity nestled in the greenery.

An olive tree surrounded by a border of Lavandula angustifolia, Rosmarinus officinalis, *and* Teucrium fruticans *marks the entrance to the garden.*
The paths and rest areas are paved with squared stones recovered from ancient pavements.

Rosemary and fronds of Sophora japonica.

Opposite
Sophora trees provide shade to the ancient stone paving at the entrance to the garden.

pp. 132–133
The garden at dawn bathed in thermal vapors. The stone building dating back to the second half of the fourteenth century, completely covered in climbing plants, is slightly lower than the terraced floor demarcated by a mixed Mediterranean border of Cistus, Rosmarinus officinalis, Lavandula angustifolia, Teucrium fruticans, Iris, Convolvulus cneorum, *and* Santolina chamaecyparissus.

TREES

Acer campestre
Arbutus unedo
Cercis siliquastrum
Cupressus sempervirens
Diospyros kaki
Eriobotrya japonica
Ficus carica
Fraxinus ornus
Morus alba
Olea europaea
Prunus avium
Prunus avium "Plena"
Punica granatum
Quercus ilex
Quercus pubescens
Sophora japonica
Sorbus domestica
Ziziphus jujuba

SHRUBS, SUBSHRUBS

Abelia x grandiflora "Prostrate White"
Aloysia citrodora
Ceanothus prostratus
Ceanothus thyrsiflorus var. *repens*
Cistus albidus f. *albus*
Cistus x purpureus
Convolvulus cneorum
Cornus mas
Corylus avellana
Helichrysum italicum
Hippocrepis emerus
Hyssopus officinalis
Laurus nobilis
Lavandula angustifolia
Lavandula angustifolia "Munstead"
Origanum majorana
Origanum vulgare
Osmanthus fragrans
Osmanthus heterophyllus
Pistacia lentiscus
Rhaphiolepis indica "Springtime"
Rosa "Cornelia"
Rosa "Nevada"
Rosmarinus officinalis
Rosmarinus officinalis
"Jackman's Prostratus"
Rosmarinus officinalis
"Tuscan Blue"
Ruta graveolens
Salvia officinalis
Santolina chamaecyparissus
Satureja montana
Spartium junceum
Syringa vulgaris
Teucrium fruticans
Thymus vulgaris
Veronica "Autumn Glory"
Viburnum opulus
Viburnum tinus

CLIMBERS

Lonicera periclymenum
Rosa banksiae "Lutea"
Trachelospermum
jasminoides

GRASSES, PERENNIAL GRASSES

Allium schoenoprasum
Foeniculum vulgare
Iris germanica
Melissa officinalis
Mentha x piperita
Nepeta x faassenii

A bronze sculpture by Ossip Zadkine, a famous twentieth-century French artist, marks the entrance to the house.

Opposite
The pergola in debarked chestnut wood is covered in climbers such as Trachelospermum jasminoides *and* Rosa banksiae "Lutea."

pp. 136 and 137
The southern side of the garden, marked off by a low border of Viburnum tinus, *overlooks the ancient thermal bath of Bagno Vignoni.*

A detail of the cast iron benches chosen for the garden's open-air resting areas.

Opposite
Flanked by Viburnum tinus, *this rustic staircase made out of railroad ties leads to the "reconstructed" woodland of native species.*

pp. 140–141
The twisted trunks of Quercus pubescens *stand out against the dawn mist: together with the holm oak, this xerophilous species is the mainstay of the Val d'Orcia woods.*

The boules green in the re-naturalized portion of the garden with native downy oak, holm oak, field maple, and strawberry tree, and shrubs such as Viburnum tinus, Pistacia lentiscus, Spartium junceum, *and* Hippocrepis emerus.

Opposite, clockwise from top left
The leaves and fruits of Sorbus domestica *in the orchard, as well as* Acer campestre, Quercus pubescens, *and* Arbutus unedo *in the "woods."*

MARCIANA MARINA [LIVORNO], TUSCANY, 2017

THE TOPIARY & **THE MEDITERRANEAN SCRUB**

Designed to complement a villa in the hills of Marciana Marina, this garden on Elba Island is the most radical example of landscape taking over the garden. In it, the wild and rugged elements of the Mediterranean scrub are not just passing references in a cultured and eclectic game. On the contrary, it is the scrub itself that becomes the identifying feature of a garden that, by being left to its naturally wild development, works as a romantic counterpoint to the extreme rationalism of the house.

The driveway to the villa is lined with stone pine, which, together with Pinus pinaster *and* Pinus halepensis, *represent the artificial pine woods that were planted between the 1950s and 1970s on Elba Island.*
Topiaries of Mediterranean species define the spaces around the house. In the background, a view of the sea.

In the immediate vicinity of the house, whose blinding white color and stacked cubes recall the feeling of a typical Mediterranean village dropping sheer into the sea, the garden apes the austere and geometric language of the architecture. A parterre of Westringia cut into spheres, clearly inspired by the tradition of Italian formal gardens, flanks the path that leads to the entrance of the house, while the hedges of holm oak, myrtle, lentisk, and laurustinus—pruned and kept low so as to not obstruct the view of the sea and surrounding woods—define the space around the house. However, the garden reaches its highest expression and originality as one moves away from the residence and ventures through the paths that snake across the scrubland.

To the east, a winding path cuts through the vegetation and leads to a round clearing with a hemispherical iron pergola-cum-sculpture from which it is possible to admire the view. Likewise to the west, another path flanked by a topiary of Mediterranean species cuts through the holm oak wood and leads to the tennis court, where an amphitheater made of concrete tiers welcomes visitors with yet another spectacular view of the sea. It is, however, in the very midst of the scrub that the eye is left free to wander and can lose itself in the beauty of the magnificent twisted trunks of the strawberry trees, mastic trees, and tree heathers, the roots of which were once used to make pipes.

Apart from the odd intervention to clear the underbrush and prune the hedges close to the villa, the garden is mostly left to its natural development and requires minimal maintenance and watering.

Opposite
The main staircase to the villa with three specimens of cypress and a parterre of Westringia fruticosa *on both sides.*

pp. 148–149
Sphere-pruned Westringia fruticosa. *This Australian plant is very similar to rosemary and has the same climatic and edaphic needs. It adapts very well to topiary.*

The amphitheater with concrete steps welcomes tennis lovers, who can also enjoy a spectacular view of the sea.

Opposite
Outside the house, hedges of Mediterranean species–holm oak, myrtle, mastic, and laurustinus–are pruned so as not to block the view of the sea.

pp. 152–153
The sunset highlights the twisted trunks of Erica arborea, *which is endemic to Elba Island, and the floristic composition of its Mediterranean scrub.*

The retaining walls were built in the traditional way (with dry stones) to allow the upper terrace to drain naturally.

A winding path runs through the Mediterranean scrub to the east. The sculptural trunks of strawberry tree, heather, and mastic tree form a very fascinating tunnel of plants.

pp. 156–157
The circular space with the hemispherical pergola-cum-sculpture in a clearing of the Quercus ilex *scrub forest. This typically Elban plant formation features many species:* Arbutus unedo, Erica arborea, Pistacia lentiscus, *as well as* Rhamnus alaternus, Myrtus communis, *and* Viburnum tinus.

SHRUBS, SUBSHRUBS

Helichrysum petiolare
Hyssopus officinalis
Laurus nobilis
Nerium oleander
Origanum majorana
Pistacia lentiscus
Plumbago auriculata
Rosmarinus officinalis
Rosmarinus officinalis "Prostratus"
Ruta graveolens
Salvia officinalis
Salvia officinalis "Purpurascens"
Santolina chamaecyparissus
Satureja montana
Teucrium fruticans
Thymus citriodorus
Westringia fruticosa

GRASSES, PERENNIAL GRASSES

Allium schoenoprasum
Artemisia absinthium
Centranthus ruber var. *coccineus*
Fragaria vesca
Melissa officinalis
Mentha x piperita
Nepeta "Six Hills Giant"
Ocimum basilicum
Petroselinum crispum

A terraced vegetable garden was built on the eastern side of the villa. The flower beds are made out of chestnut poles.

Opposite
An isolated specimen of Pinus pinaster *towers over the holm oak scrub, with the sea in the background.*

CAPALBIO [GROSSETO], TUSCANY, 2008

THE MAREMMA & THE CORK OAK

The Maremma, and the whole area south of Grosseto in particular, is undoubtedly one of the most fascinating and wild Italian landscapes. In agreement with the client, who asked Anna to "not cut his view from this sea of green," the garden of Capalbio takes on an almost ancillary role with respect to the surrounding landscape, so that the eye, left to roam freely, can surrender to the allure and beauty of the panorama.

The villa's internal courtyard with its long pool running down the center. Four bitter orange trees were planted symmetrically on either side. One wall of the building is entirely covered by Parthenocissus tricuspidata "Veitchii." *In the background, the western side of the garden offers a magnificent view of the Maremma landscape.*

When the owners purchased it, the garden was but a very large area of just about two-and-a-half acres with a limited number of trees: a few oaks, a few olive trees, and a big fig tree leaning directly against an agricultural annex. The intervention, unlike in other cases, was aimed at not overturning this view but rather preserving it, so that the greenery wouldn't obstruct the surroundings and the garden itself could almost act as a "terrace" opening onto the farmland all around.

The garden is enclosed by mixed borders of subshrubs, Mediterranean herbaceous perennials, and grasses such as rock rose, helichrysum, Jerusalem sage, fescue, and lovegrass that blend with the wild prairie outside. As for the trees, the choice fell mostly on native species, which were selected over numerous visits to a famous Tuscan nursery. Cork oaks with twisted trunks (endemic in this area due to its particular microclimate), oaks, field maples, holm oaks, and strawberry trees were carefully handpicked for their specific shapes to ensure they would resemble as closely as possible those punctuating the landscape. In particular, the field maples, which, pruned in the iconic candelabra shapes, used to hold up the "married vine" (*vite maritata*), were chosen as evidence of this old method of cultivation, the origins of which hark back to the Etruscans.

As seen elsewhere, the area near the house is characterized by the presence of "architectural" elements, such as the large vegetable garden housing fruit trees and flower beds, or yet other features typical of Italian formal gardens, like the water pond. However, the heart of the garden is the area to the west, its rustic quality contrasting beautifully with the contemporary design furniture chosen by the homeowner. Planned so that the vista can be enjoyed year-round, the "outdoor living room," formed by a terracotta flooring and two chestnut-wood pergolas to each side, gives its best at dusk, when the garden and the Maremma surroundings are bathed in orange.

An old specimen of field maple, with its characteristic candelabra shape, bears witness to the usage of vite maritata*, an ancient method of vine cultivation whose origins date back to the Etruscans.*

Detail of the mixed border that winds along the perimeter of the garden, with olive trees, grasses, and Helichrysum italicum.

Opposite
The colors of the Mediterranean suffruticoses Phlomis futicosa *and* Helichrysum italicum *blend into the surrounding countryside.*

pp. 166–167
The western side of the garden at sunset. A low border of Gaura lindheimeri *and* Verbena bonariensis, *as well as grasses and Mediterranean perennials, snakes along the perimeter of the garden and merges with the wild field beyond.*

The infinity pool at sunset. The north side of the swimming pool is paved with ancient stones laid between the grass and furnished with brightly colored chaise longues. The garden is a "window" that opens onto the surrounding countryside.

Opposite
Grasses and Gaura lindheimeri *surround the ancient stone steps leading to the swimming pool.*

Two cork trees with twisted trunks. The trees chosen for this garden (durmast, field maple, holm oak, manna ash, and strawberry tree) come from a famous Tuscan nursery and are typical of the Maremma.

Opposite
Ancient reclaimed stones anchored to the wall of an old agricultural depot lend an air of privacy to the open-air showers.

pp. 172–173
The "outdoor living room" with the terracotta flooring and one of the two chestnut wood pergolas on the west side of the house, with contemporary furnishings chosen by the lady of the house. The perfect place to enjoy the wonderful Maremma sunsets.

A rustic pergola with wooden furnishings and comfortable cushions for total relaxation. The Capalbio villa has numerous outdoor areas that must never be missing in a garden.

Opposite
A manna ash–a species widespread throughout the peninsula and islands–grows next to the pergola with Rosa bracteata "Mermaid" *and* Lippia citrodora *nestling below.*

Specimens of cork, oak, and cypress border the garden on the western side.

Opposite
The pergola on the northwestern side. An old field maple and an olive tree frame the wonderful landscape.

pp. 178 and 179
The large (nearly 200-square-yard) vegetable garden was planted on the northern side of the house. It is surrounded by a rosemary hedge and its paths are made of rustic tuff bricks. The geometric vegetable beds alternate with beds of flowers and cut roses.

TREES

Acer campestre
Acer monspessulanum
Arbutus unedo
Cercis siliquastrum
Citrus x aurantium
Cupressus sempervirens
Cydonia oblonga
Eriobotrya japonica
Ficus carica
Fraxinus ornus
Laburnum anagyroides
Melia azedarach
Olea europaea
Prunus amygdalus
Prunus armeniaca
Punica granatum
Pyrus pyraster
Quercus ilex
Quercus pubescens
Quercus suber

SHRUBS, SUBSHRUBS

Aloysia citrodora
Artemisia arborescens
Cistus albidus f. *albus*
Cistus x purpureus
Citrus x limon
Cornus mas
Cornus sanguinea
Crataegus monogyna
Helichrysum italicum
Juniperus communis
Malva x clementii "Rosea"
Myrtus communis
Myrtus communis subsp. *tarentina*
Perovskia atriplicifolia "Blue Spire"
Phillyrea angustifolia
Phlomis fruticosa
Pistacia lentiscus
Pseudodictamnus mediterraneus
Rhamnus alaternus
Rosa "Abraham Darby"
Rosa canina
Rosa "Chianti"
Rosa "Evelyn"
Rosa "Falstaff"
Rosa "Golden Celebration"
Rosa "William Shakespeare"
Rosmarinus officinalis
Salvia leucantha
Salvia microphylla "Pink Blush"
Salvia microphylla "Royal Bumble"
Spartium junceum
Teucrium fruticans "Azureum"
Vitex agnus-castus
Westringia fruticosa

CLIMBERS

Jasminum mesnyi
Lonicera caprifolium
Parthenocissus tricuspidata "Veitchii"
Rosa "Mermaid"
Trachelospermum asiaticum

GRASSES, PERENNIAL GRASSES

Calamagrostis x acutiflora "Karl Foerster"
Centranthus ruber "Albus"
Centranthus ruber var. *coccineus*
Eragrostis curvula
Euphorbia characias
Festuca filiformis
Gaura lindheimeri
Iris pallida
Leymus arenarius
Nepeta "Six Hills Giant"
Panicum virgatum "Heavy Metal"
Pennisetum alopecuroides "Hameln"
Poa labillardierei
Verbena bonariensis

Hydrangea arborescens "Annabelle" *and* Iris pallida *on the small slope. An enormous fig tree grows next to the old stone cottage.*

Opposite
The pool in the courtyard. Next to the wall covered in Canadian vine, two lemon trees in terracotta pots.

1,263 **feet** ASL

PASSIGNANO SUL TRASIMENO [PERUGIA], UMBRIA, 2001–04

THE TERRACE
& THE LAKE

Originally conceived as the green space of an *hôtel de charme* connecting the house (an old Capuchin convent dating back to 1456) and Lake Trasimeno to the south, the garden of Passignano, now part of a private residence, is another example of a landscape intervention where architectural elements of the Italian formal garden are revisited so that it opens up and blends with the woods above and the olive groves below.

The geometric design of the southern portion of the garden with rows of olive trees and pergolas of grapes is enhanced by the dark green of the cypresses marking the border. In the background, Lake Trasimeno in all its charm.

Mediterranean mixed borders of rockrose, rosemary, helichrysum, and myrtle define the house and flank the slopes and retaining walls connecting the different levels of the garden. To the east, a water pond draws attention to the holm oak wood, while to the south a cross-shaped vegetable garden surrounded by boxwood hedges and with the prerequisite sundial in the center leads first to a double pergola conceived to recover the grapevines originally planted on the north side, and, further on, to the hemispherical iron pergola, which, functioning as a belvedere in the southwest corner, offers a charming view of the lake.

Worth highlighting is also the presence of five rows of lavender—a Provençal touch—which, arranged in parallel pairs, create frothy gray-on-gray bushes that integrate perfectly with the olive trees, cypress trees, and other fruit trees that have been mostly preserved or, in a few instances, planted.

"The original owner who commissioned the garden envisaged a number of furnished areas to create a sort of outdoor living room, but then gave me *carte blanche*," says Anna. And indeed, what catches the eye and gives the garden its romantic atmosphere is the play of perspectives and volumes between the different plants that overlap and then merge with the surroundings. In particular, the preexisting olive grove, referenced in the layout of both the double pergola and the lavender borders, has become an integral part of the garden. An intervention inspired by the ordered and man-made environment of Central Italy, but which softens some of its rigid rules and geometries, for a result in which learned nods and references exalt the freedom and elegance of the design.

Opposite
The pergola of debarked chestnut poles. Lavender topiary in the lawn. In the background, rosemary covering the slopes of the garden alongside other drought-resistant plants.

pp. 186–187
The garden of the Passignano convent set in a typically Italian landscape–the holm oak grove to the east and the gentle forms of the olive groves and vineyards.

The olive trees of the convent blend into the Umbrian landscape.
The lake can be seen beyond the cypresses and stone pine.

Opposite
Five double rows of lavender run through the olive grove, connecting the designed part of the garden and the preexisting olive grove.

pp. 190–191
The lavender topiary creates foams of gray on gray and blends perfectly with the olive trees, cypresses, and fruit trees, which were maintained or in a few cases planted.

The greenhouse, once a suite of the hôtel de charme *and now used as a fitness room, offers an enchanting view of the olive grove on one side and Lake Trasimeno on the other.*

Opposite
Interwoven with old, transplanted vines, wisteria, and roses, a long pergola arranged in parallel rows extends along the southern side of the garden, leading to the greenhouse and the belvedere.

pp. 194–195
A mixed border with Gaura lindheimeri *marks off the open-air living rooms next to the convent building. The southern side of the garden offers lavender hedges, olive trees, and fruit trees. The double pergola entirely embraced by climbing plants provides pleasant shade during the hot Umbrian summers.*

The iron belvedere pergola with Rosa banksiae "Lutea" *and the brazier in the center: the amazing sunsets can be enjoyed year-round.*

Opposite
Clouds above Lake Trasimeno create magical reflections on the water.

pp. 198–199
An iron pergola shades one of the open-air living rooms built close to the walls of the convent, as the first owner desired. A staircase of local stone leads to the terraced level of the swimming pool.

Enclosed by a box hedge, the vegetable garden is divided into four flower beds by paths paved with local terracotta bricks. In the center, a sundial with stone base.

Opposite
The southern side of the convent with pergolas and lavender hedges. A mixed border of drought-resistant plants, Agapanthus campanulatus, Gaura, Convolvulus cneorum, Malva x clementii "Rosea," Thymus "Porlock" *marks off the tastefully decorated pergola shaded by climbers.*

pp. 202–203
A containing wall made of local stone separates the large flat lawn from the holm oak grove above. A blade of water falls from the upper floor into the large rectangular basin. Drought-resistant Mediterranean plants such as Rosmarinus officinalis "Prostratus," Teucrium fruticans, Helichrysum italicum, Cistus, Phlomis, *and* Myrtus communis *grow on the slopes beyond the wall.*

TREES
Arbutus unedo
Cupressus sempervirens
Juglans regia
Malus domestica "Annurca"
Morus platanifolia
Olea europaea
Prunus amygdalus
Prunus armeniaca
Prunus avium
Punica granatum
Ziziphus jujuba

SHRUBS, SUBSHRUBS
Arbutus unedo "Compacta"
Buxus microphylla "Faulkner"
Buxus sempervirens
Buxus sempervirens "Suffruticosa"
Caryopteris x clandonensis "Heavenly Blue"
Ceanothus "Concha"
Ceanothus griseus var. *horizontalis* "Yankee Point"
Ceanothus "Italian Skies"
Ceanothus prostratus
Ceanothus "Skylark"
Ceanothus thyrsiflorus var. *repens*
Cistus albidus f. *albus*
Cistus x argenteus "Peggy Sammons"
Cistus x purpureus
Cistus x skanbergii
Citrus trifoliata
Convolvulus cneorum
Convolvulus sabatius
Cytisus battandieri
Feijoa sellowiana
Genista lydia
Helichrysum italicum subsp. *serotinum*
Helichrysum petiolare
Hippocrepis emerus
Hydrangea paniculata "Limelight"
Hydrangea paniculata "Unique"
Jasminum mesnyi
Lavandula angustifolia
Lavandula angustifolia "Hidcote"
Lavandula x intermedia "Grosso"
Malva x clementii "Rosea"
Myrtus communis
Myrtus communis subsp. *tarentina*
Perovskia atriplicifolia "Blue Spire"
Phillyrea angustifolia
Phlomis fruticosa
Pseudodictamnus mediterraneus
Rhaphiolepis indica "Springtime"
Rosa "Ballerina"
Rosa "Buff Beauty"
Rosa "Cornelia"
Rosa "Felicia"
Rosa "Ice Meidiland"
Rosa "Marguerite Hilling"
Rosa x odorata "Mutabilis"
Rosa x odorata "Sanguinea"
Rosa "Penelope"
Rosa "Schneeflocke"
Rosa "Sea Foam"
Rosa "White Meidiland"
Rosmarinus officinalis
Rosmarinus officinalis "Jackman's Prostratus"
Rosmarinus officinalis "Prostratus"
Rosmarinus officinalis "Rampant Boule"
Rosmarinus officinalis "Tuscan Blue"
Ruscus aculeatus
Santolina chamaecyparissus
Solanum rantonnetii
Teucrium fruticans
Teucrium fruticans "Azureum"
Thymus "Porlock"
Thymus vulgaris
Viburnum tinus
Viburnum tinus "Eve Price"
Vitex agnus-castus
Westringia fruticosa

CLIMBERS
Hedera helix
Jasminum officinale
Rosa banksiae "Lutea"
Rosa "Crimson Glory"
Rosa "Gloire de Dijon"
Rosa "Nahema"
Rosa "Souvenir de Claudius Denoyel"
Rosa "Souvenir du Docteur Jamain"
Vitis vinifera
Wisteria sinensis
Wisteria sinensis f. *alba*
Wisteria sinensis "Prolific"

GRASSES, PERENNIAL GRASSES
Acanthus spinosus
Agapanthus campanulatus
Centranthus ruber var. *coccineus*
Gaura lindheimeri
Iris germanica
Nepeta racemosa "Walker's Low"
Nepeta "Six Hills Giant"

Quercus ilex, *an evergreen oak, is typical to the Mediterranean forest. In the Passignano garden, the holm oak is maintained with great care.*

OSTUNI [BRINDISI], APULIA, 2021–22

THE TUFF & THE OLIVE TREE

Nestled in the plain that leads from the town to the sea, the garden of Ostuni is the prototype of landscape design for an era in which climate change and global warming have made water scarcity and drought an ever-present reality. Surrounded by centuries-old olive trees and a low wall in local tuff that defines its perimeter, this garden is a clear homage to Apulia: it appropriates the most evocative and picturesque features of the region's landscape and integrates them with more contemporary elements.

View of the farmstead from above. The garden is surrounded by low walls in tuff stone. Inside, serpentines of drought-resistant grasses and trees typical to Apulia, such as olive, carob, cork, fig, and pomegranate. The lawn was replaced by a crushed stone flooring.

Within the low tuff walls, mixed borders of drought-resistant grasses alternating exotic and native varieties (which, even at their maximum height, never grow taller than the barriers) develop in sinuous serpentines that, swaying in the wind, merge with the wild prairie on the other side. The few trees that were planted, selected to reflect the surrounding landscape, are on the contrary quintessentially Mediterranean: the indispensable olive trees alternate with carobs, cork oaks, pomegranate trees, and fig trees, while the two pergolas are dressed with old vines of local table grapes.

The selection of the single varieties was discussed with and agreed to by the owner, Antonia Giacinti, a renowned fashion entrepreneur hailing from Milan, who accompanied Anna on her visits to the nursery and collaborated actively in the choice of the plants, from the individual grasses and shrubs all the way to the exemplary trees. "It's always a pleasure when the clients come with me to the nursery, because this way they get enthusiastically involved and start to look at the choices behind designing a garden in a different light. Plus, Antonia has excellent taste," says Anna.

The absolute harmony between the vision of the designer, the desires of the owner, and the inherent limits of a context characterized by extreme salinity and lack of water resulted in the decision to forgo a lawn. This was replaced by a crushed stone flooring that mirrors the color of the tuff of the farmstead—which from rural ruin has been turned into a contemporary summer residence—and elevates the sinuous volumes of the mixed borders. The result, at once elegant and beautiful, is the perfect example of the garden of the future, which looks to the world for inspiration but whose design choices are deeply rooted in the local landscape.

The wall in local tuff stone at the southern end of the garden.
A mixed border of Poa labilladierei *and* Stipa ichu
opens the view onto the Ostuni plain.

The farmstead, with its red-painted tuff stone, was restored by architect Francesca Neri Antonello. In the background, mixed borders of grasses and Mediterranean plants, such as Ephorbia characias subsp. wulfenii, Thymbra capitata, Eryngium planum "Silver Salentino," *and* Echinops ritro "Platinum Blue," *merge into the wild prairie beyond the tuff wall.*

Opposite
A carob tree grows in the border of Stipa tenuissima, Perovskia atriplicifolia "Blue Spire," *and* Pennisetum. *In the background, a cluster of prickly pear cacti.*

An olive tree with twisted trunk marks the edge of the garden between the Stipa ichu *and the wild-growing prairie.*

Opposite
The pool is enclosed by a border of grasses, in particular, Eragrostis elliottii, Poa labillardierei, *and* Stipa ichu, *which ripple in the wind for an extremely charming effect.*

pp. 214–215
On the southern side of the pool is a mixed grass border with Andropogon scoparius "Camper," Stipa tenuissima, Eragrostis elliottii, Pennisetum, *and* Mischanthus. *On the north side, a large pergola with old local table grape vines.*

Close to the western wall of the farmstead, an ancient pomegranate tree, with its twisted branches, shows off its rich fruit.

Opposite
Festuca mairei *and* Andropogon scoparius "Camper."
Farmed fields extend beyond the border wall to the north, while the sea glistens in the background.

TREES
Ceratonia siliqua
Ficus carica
Olea europaea
Punica granatum
Quercus suber

SHRUBS, SUBSHRUBS
Artemisia abrotanum
Convolvulus cneorum
Euphorbia characias subsp. *wulfenii*
Helichrysum italicum
Lotus hirsutus
Opuntia ficus-indica
Perovskia atriplicifolia "Blue Spire"
Perovskia atriplicifolia "Little Spire"
Pistacia lentiscus
Pseudodictamnus hirsutus
Rosmarinus officinalis
Salvia officinalis
Salvia microphylla "Royal Bumble"
Satureja spicigera
Thymbra capitata
Thymus ciliatus

CLIMBERS
Bougainvillea "Rotana Orange"
Jasminum azoricum
Vitis vinifera

GRASSES, PERENNIAL GRASSES
Andropogon gerardii "Prairie Sommer"
Andropogon scoparius "Camper"
Chionochloa rubra
Echinops ritro "Platinum Blue"
Elymus arenarius "Ice Blue"
Elymus farctus
Eragrostis elliottii
Eryngium planum "Silver Salentino"
Euphorbia corallioides
Festuca mairei
Gaura lindheimeri
Pennisetum setaceum "Rubrum"
Poa labillardierei
Stachys byzantina
Stipa ichu
Stipa tenuissima

A rustic wooden bench surrounded by a border of grasses with Eragrostis elliottii *and* Pennisetum setaceum "Rubrum."

Opposite
Northern side of the farmstead with Festuca mairei, Artemisia abrotanum, *and* Helichrysum italicum. *A winding crushed stone pavement has replaced the lawn, which would have taken lots of care and water.*

pp. 220–221
With their wonderfully twisted trunks, the ancient olive trees create a continuum with the landscape. Fig plants complete the arboreal decoration on the northern side of the garden.

pp. 222–223
The textures and colors of the mixed borders blend with those of the landscape surrounding the farmstead. In the background, a view of the sea.

Front cover and back cover
View from above of the garden
of Marciana Marina on Elba Island

Art Direction and Graphic Design
Cristina Menotti

Translation
TperTradurre Srl

All photographs by
Matteo Carassale

Image of the leaf at the beginning of chapters
Adobe Stock
X-ray image of coleus leaf
by Connect Images

Texts by
Bartolomeo Sala

Distributed in English throughout the World by
Rizzoli International Publications, Inc.
49 West 27th Street
New York, NY 10001
www.rizzoliusa.com

ISBN: 978-88-918445-1-4

Printed in Italy
2025 2026 2027 2028 / 10 9 8 7 6 5 4 3 2 1

The authorized representative in the EU for safety
and compliance is Mondadori Libri S.p.A.,
via Gian Battista Vico 42, Milan, Italy, 20123,
http://www.mondadori.it

Visit us online:
Instagram.com/RizzoliBooks
Facebook.com/RizzoliNewYork
X: @Rizzoli_Books
Youtube.com/user/RizzoliNY